How
To
Homeschool
(Yes, You!)

by

Julia Toto

Huntington House Publishers
P.O. Box 53788
Lafayette, Louisiana 70505

Library of Congress Card Catalog Number
93-80619
ISBN 1-56384-059-6

Contents

Chapter One

Home Education

"What's it all about? Is it legal? Where do I begin? Am I qualified? Where do I find the right books? Who can help me? What do I tell my mother-in-law?" Sound familiar? Relax, you're not alone. We all start out just like you—eager, nervous, and sometimes overwhelmed. All these questions have answers! We'll take them one at a time and even cover things you may not have thought to ask. So, pour yourself a cup of coffee and let's talk about home education.

First of all, let me congratulate you for taking this first step—inquiring. The largest contributing factor to misunderstanding is ignorance, the second is misinformation. While the reasons for and methods of home education tend to vary, a basic understanding is crucial for parents wanting to make informed choices.

Teaching our children at home demands honest commitment. We strive for academic excellence, yet home education goes far beyond just teaching the three Rs. It is a serious decision to nurture and train our children to be the very best they can be in every area of life. Home education provides an opportunity to develop a child's full potential—spiritually, emotionally, physically, as well as, academically.

Home education is an alternative lifestyle that leads to a lifelong love of learning. Life itself becomes the classroom. Research and "book learning" are vital, but the real test comes when a child is able to apply the knowledge he or she has learned to everyday situations. Critical thinking skills are exercised, and children experience first-hand the principles of cause and effect. Learning continues long after the school books are put away for the day.

But, is it legal? Yes! Your right to educate your child at home, according to your convictions, is protected under the United States Constitution. The First Amendment guarantees free exercise of religion. The right to liberty and privacy are guaranteed under the Fourteenth Amendment. However, laws regulating home education do vary from state to state. It is your responsibility as parents to know and comply with your state's laws. Most are clearly defined and easily followed. New legislation is being introduced all the time, and it is advantageous to join your state home education organization. Together, families can keep informed of issues pertinent to their children's welfare.

The Home School Legal Defense Association offers legal assistance on a membership basis. HSLDA proposes to help homeschool members who may run into problems and legal snags due to inconsistent rulings of state laws. We encourage new families to join. To obtain a copy of your state's homeschool laws, or if you would like a membership application for HSLDA, you may contact them at: Home School Legal Defense Association, Box 159, Paeonian Springs, VA 22129.

Chapter Two

Qualified vs. Certified

Many people question whether or not parents are qualified to teach their children at home. One cannot dismiss the obvious advantages of one-to-one tutoring over the average teacher-student ratio found in conventional classrooms. Teaching your children at home gives you that advantage. In most states, volunteer teacher aids are not required to be state certified. They are simply concerned parents, like yourself, who are able to take the necessary time with children one at a time.

It is not unusual to feel inadequate. After all, we have been led to believe that education is best left up to the "experts" once our children reach five or six years old. Recent findings show that this is not always true. One such study on home education was recently conducted in Oklahoma. Researchers gathered data from participating families across the state on family characteristics of the student, as well as academic achievement scores. The average score of students who had been taught at home was at or above the 82d percentile in reading, listening, language, math, and science. Dr. Brian Ray of the National Home Education Research Institute reported the study also revealed "there was no significant relationship between achievement and the variables of parent education level, whether parents had been certified teachers, age of student, hours of formal education per day, and number of children in the family."[1]

Certification and qualification are two different things. Do you realize you have already filled the qualification of being your children's teacher for many years before they became "school age"? You have been their first and most important teacher. You have taught them how to walk, communicate, eat, dress, share, use the bathroom, and tie their shoes; this only touches the list of skills they have learned from you. You have worked side by side with your children instructing, counseling, and disciplining them. As a parent, you have nursed and nurtured your children like no one else could. You have laughed, cried, and already learned a lot together. Do you think teaching them to sound out letters or add numbers is really all that different?

You see, we've been convinced that we are incapable of finishing what we have already started. Academics are very important, and an exciting part of your children's development, but they are only one part of a very big, beautiful picture in which you have already had the privilege of being a very crucial factor. Dr. Raymond Moore is a renowned psychologist and founder of Hewitt Research Foundation. His wife, Dorothy, is an educator and reading specialist. The Moores have suggested that the best teachers may not even know who they are. While a degree of higher education is to be applauded, evidence of a good teacher is not always noted by a big desk, a red pencil, or a neatly framed certificate. In their book, *Home Style Teaching*, the Moores describe the best teacher as one who is "aware of the crucial interaction of adult and child feelings, and who provides a responsive, understanding, inspiring, emotional sanctuary for the students. Thus, most of the spectacular teaching results we have seen in nearly fifty professional years have involved both rural and urban parents, mainly without college degrees and usually without much confidence, but with a lot of love."[2] With encouraging people like the Moores, the right curriculum, a testing service to watch your child's academic progress, and many good resources available, you will soon regain your confidence to continue teaching your child. So, to answer your question: yes, mom, and dad, you do qualify.

Chapter Three

Why in the World?

———————— ✍ ————————

According to a 1990 synopsis by the Home School Legal Defense Association, there are an estimated 630,000 children in homeschooling families across the United States. Why would parents choose this option when their hard earned tax dollars already pay for public schools to do the job for them? This question may have as many different answers as there are families! Let's explore a few of the most common reasons.

Shortly after his inauguration, President and Mrs. Clinton announced that they would enroll their daughter in a private school. The news was quite controversial, and the First Family was put in the position of having to publicly justify this very personal decision. They could not allow the media or the voting public to stand in the way of their parental rights and responsibilities. The nation was informed by the Clintons, and rightly so, that they MUST do what they feel is best for their

daughter. Well put. The same rights and responsibilities belong to each one of us. We
choose to home educate because we, too,
must do what is best for our children. Reasons for choosing private education are left
to the conscience of individual families.
However, many people find the high cost of
tuition beyond their budget. While home
education still requires significant funding,
it is far less expensive than most private
schools. This is especially true for families
with more than one child. The vast majority
of families who decide to teach their children at home do so after much prayer. Their
decision is a matter of spiritual conviction.
However, Christians are not the only ones
homeschooling their children these days.
Many parents feel the public schools no
longer serve the best interest of their students. While we may not agree on the problem or the solution, Americans willingly
admit something is drastically wrong with
our educational system, and no amount of
money will cure it.

Just one generation ago, classroom di-
versions included gum chewing, paper wads,
tardiness, and smoking in the boys restroom.
Times have changed. Today's educators must
be prepared to deal with aggravated assault,
gangs, guns, knives, and crack. The growing
ranks of unmotivated, undisciplined young

people tax the effectiveness of even the most caring teachers and administrators. Crime is not the only malady inflicting our young people. Morality has become relevant in our contemporary society. Students and teachers alike are forced to confront pre-marital sex, unprepared pregnancies, homosexuality, abortion, and the top 40 STDs (Sexually Transmitted Diseases). What's happening in the classroom, unfortunately, may only be a reflection of our society's condition as a whole.

Such issues are often not looked upon as problems, but rather as normal contemporary issues. Reform measures often include sex education at younger grades, condom distribution, and school-based health clinics. Statistics now prove that these "remedies" only add fuel to a wildfire. Many teachers are finding it progressively difficult to teach basic academic skills under such conditions, and understandably so. Since 1962, test scores across the nation have consistently plunged, while teen pregnancies and STDs have soared. It is interesting to note that this was the very year that prayer was banned from the public classrooms in America by the Supreme Court. A coincidence? Not likely.

Another concern parents have is that their children have become pawns in a tax-funded chess game. Political and social agendas have taken their seat in American classrooms for some time now. There are often subtle underlying philosophies propagated in the classroom that many people, including teachers, may be unaware of. In a nation that has boasted of educational excellence, we have remained dangerously ignorant of the course our learning institutions are on.

A leading constituent of our schools' present condition is a man named John Dewey. In 1930 Dewey, who had been a professor of philosophy at several American universities, resigned his position from the University of Columbia, and at seventy-one years old, dedicated the last twenty-two years of his life to the cause of liberalism in politics. In his book, *En Route To Global Occupation*, author Gary Kah states:

> Dewey, who became known as the "father of progressive education," went on to influence the thinking of American educators more than any other individual. What few people realize about Dewey is that he was one of America's leading atheists. He wrote: "There is no God and no soul. Hence, there are no needs for the props of traditional religion. With dogma and creed excluded, then immutable (unchangeable) truth is also dead and buried. There is no room for fixed, natural law or permanent moral absolutes."[1]

Is it any wonder this father of educational reform has sired a generation of high school graduates, many of whom cannot read their diplomas?

Any remnant of academic standards that does remain is quickly being smothered by such reformation attempts as "outcome-based" education. This type of curriculum is less concerned with the child's academic progress (or lack of it) than with how well the child attains to behavior standards established in the curriculum. One question: whose standards?

The National Education Association is gaining ominous control in the operations and attitudes of America's public schools. What seemingly began as an organization of concerned educators promoting quality education took a turn in the 1970s to that of a politically aggressive labor union.

Reader's Digest quotes former NEA president Mary Futrell, "Instruction and professional development have been on the back burner to us compared with political action."[2] According to the same article, local and state teacher's associations are rising up to challenge many of the NEA's cohesive intentions to promote their liberal ideas in the classroom. Professor Chester E. Finn, Jr., of Vanderbilt University, made the following comment upon his analysis of the NEA's material:

> It includes the delegitimizing of all author-
> ity save that of the state, the degradation of
> traditional morality, and the encouragement
> of citizens in general and children in par-
> ticular to despise the rules and customs that
> make their society a functional democracy.
> The NEA is drifting into exceedingly dan-
> gerous waters, and probably carrying more
> than a few teachers and pupils with it. Well
> meaning dedicated teachers may find them-
> selves unwittingly being used to promote
> values that many parents do not espouse.[3]

The context of tax-funded school textbooks has become progressively controversial. Ask yourself, "If my child does learn to
read, does it matter **what** he reads? As long
as he's passing history and science, does it
really matter if the subject material is accu-
rate?" Of course it should matter. Unfortunately, to some parents, as well as professional educators, the end justifies the means.

George Washington once said, "Truth
will ultimately prevail where there is pains
taken to bring it to light." Yet contemporary
textbooks seem to take great pains to hide
the truth by ignoring historical facts. History
does not lie, yet the authors of our public
school's curriculum often delete the provi-

dential shaping of events which have taken place throughout our nation's history. For nearly two centuries our schools' textbooks were written in light of God's authorative Word. Now, textbooks which propagate hypothetical evolutionary theories, new age teaching, and historical misinformation are being used in classrooms all across America. Left in the wake of their humanistic world view is a generation of citizens ignorant of our true godly heritage, and blind to the snares set before us.

Americans are becoming increasingly aware of the political essence of modern educational reforms and can no longer ignore the facts. When the values in the classroom differ from those of a child's family, it causes the child to unnecessarily choose one authority over the other. Taking back responsibility for their children's education and standing up for their own family values may be one step toward the restoration of America's godly foundation. Mike Fueslier, author of *America Awaiting the Verdict* says, "The anarchy and decimation we are experiencing in society today is just the beginning . . . unless we return to our Christian roots—we are finished."[4]

We extol and pray for those godly teachers who are on the front lines in our schools. While the demoralizing of our public education system is a major contributing factor to the growing ranks of home educators, it would be unfair to say that all home-schoolers have had bad experiences with the public schools. On the contrary, some have had very good experiences, and yet they have simply chosen what was best over what was good.

Academic excellence is a goal of all families involved in home education, and most strive to build strong, godly character as well. To many, even the option of private school cannot replace the quality of love, training, and instruction a child receives at home. Children are a blessing. Each one is a gift from God. He has given them to us to love and enjoy, to nurture and train, and we are ultimately accountable to Him for how we have raised them.

We live in a nation that has become very conscious of the environment. We stress the importance of good stewardship of this earth, and each of us desires to do our part to take care of the natural resources God has provided for our use. How much more seriously should we take our stewardship of His most precious creation, our children who are made in His image.

Sound instructions are given to us as parents in God's Word, but perhaps one passage rings loud and clear through the hearts of many homeschoolers. Deuteronomy 6:4-7 says:

> Hear, O' Israel, the Lord our God, the Lord is one! Thou shalt love the Lord thy God with all thine heart, and with all thy soul, and with all thy might. And these words which I command thee this day shall be in thine heart; and thou shalt teach them diligently unto thy children, and shalt talk of them when thou sittest in thine house, and when thou walkest by the way, when thou liest down, and when thou risest up. (KJV)

God is telling us to remember Him, to teach His commandments to our children, not just in church, but always. We need to live out God's ways in all we do and to do everything in light of His Word. God loves us, and there is no part of our lives that He is not intimately aware of. He is with us always and always ready to lead, teach, and help us, if we'll ask—even with math!

Chapter Four

One Family's Story

---- ✍ ----

The elementary school in our Mid-Western suburb was a welcome improvement over the public schools our child first attended out west. In fact, I thought they were exceptional. Though growing, the student-teacher ratio was much lower than other schools in our area, and my children's teachers were committed educators. I developed a good working relationship with them and truly feel they had their student's best interest at heart. Sounds pretty ideal, doesn't it? Why then would I give all that up, along with free mornings and a clean house, to teach our children at home?

My husband and I have always been actively involved in our children's education. I was on our PTA board, as well as a special committee under our local superintendent. We held coffees in our home, made phone calls, and campaigned when it was time to vote on bond money or tax increases that would directly benefit our school. We have no regrets and continue to support endeavors that will genuinely improve our local public schools. By choosing to become involved, we were forced to confront issues that many parents may ignore. No one relishes confrontation, but sometimes taking a stand for our faith requires making unpopular decisions.

God lets His heart be made known concerning many things directly related to Halloween in Deuteronomy 18:1-12. Because of this, our family chooses not to commemorate this day in our home. Yet during the entire month of October, our children's classrooms seemed pre-occupied with witches, ghosts, and vampires. Our first grader's music lessons included a dark room with sounds of human groans and eerie music. While these activities may sound quite harmless, we must remember that it is the spirit behind Halloween that makes them an abomination to the Lord. Halloween parties got so out-of-hand that one child dressed as Freddy Kruger and brought a hatchet to school. Even the teachers admitted this event was getting uglier and more destructive every year. Since the PTA funded these activities, I suggested to our board that the emphasis and allocations be shifted from Halloween parties to Thanksgiving feasts, an authentic American celebration and a good, hands-on history lesson at that! Though other parents supported my suggestion, tradition ruled, and the parties continued.

Other issues also arose. Transactional Analysis, a new age technique, was being taught in my son's fourth grade class by the guidance counselor. This was supposed to help students with their self-esteem. I knew better, and the guidance counselor should have. Though she may have meant no harm, perhaps she should have researched her material a bit further.

These were not the deciding factors in our choice to teach our children at home, although perhaps they should have been. The amount of time our oldest son was spending on homework grew every year. By the time he was in the fourth grade, he had four to five hours of homework every evening; this was after spending seven hours at school. He became discouraged, tired, and confused. Sound familiar? In spite of the fact that we had worked with our son regularly, and his teachers gave him the same amount of time they gave other students to finish the work, he fell further and further behind. Although he was in remedial math and reading classes, his achievement scores consistently averaged one to two years behind grade level. Some of the problem was due to the fact that our child had a mild hearing loss but not severe enough to be placed outside of a regular classroom. A greater handicap was that the schools he started out in did not teach phonics. Our child was losing self-respect, and his motivation was slipping to a dangerous low. After discussing it with our son, we unofficially requested he be held back a year. However, our request was denied. The school felt it was worse for a child's self-esteem to hold him back and catch up than it was to have him in the "slow group," always one step behind the crowd. There is validity to both sides of this argument, and although we had reservations, we conceded to his promotion.

Since we lived near the school it was easy to meet with his teachers on a regular basis. Sometimes it was necessary to make contact several times a week. We supported each other's plans to help my son stay on task and use his time efficiently. I have no doubt his teachers were truly doing their best to meet the needs of their growing classes. By the fourth grade, I was 'tutoring' our son for a minimum of three hours a night in math, reading, and language. Home education started sounding less and less ridiculous. "How much more difficult could it be to teach him myself?" I wondered. At least then I would have access to instructions and an answer key! The Lord had to let me see for myself that I really was an important teacher to my child already and that by trusting Him I could tackle this!

Our decision was not made overnight. Much prayerful consideration and research was done first. We realized that not only were our children beginning to learn things we didn't approve of, but we also had so little time with them at home for teaching values and practical skills that would benefit them for a lifetime. Close friends home-schooled, and we were beginning to see traits in their children, and in their home that we desired to instill in our own.

We finished the school year and decided upon home education over the summer. I'm glad that we had developed a good relationship with our children's teachers and principal and were able to discuss openly and honestly our reasons to teach at home. Our children were intimately involved in our decision-making process. They will be the first to tell you they love it, and their desire to continue their education at home is a constant source of encouragement to me. My children have fond memories of their teachers, yet there are many things about public school they are glad they no longer have to contend with. Although they miss the monkey bars at recess and greasy pizza for lunch, they are quick to point out advantages of homeschooling.

I cannot pass up this opportunity to share with you how quickly our son's attitude and self-confidence improved once we began to teach him at home. His reading and language skills went from below grade level to far above grade level after our first year. Math, which had once intimidated him to the point of tears, became one of his favorite subjects once we found the appropriate math program for him. He occasionally tutors his younger brother and sister. Yes, it's work! And yes, it works.

Though each family is unique, our story is not unusual. Time and again I listen to testimonies from parents whose child had been struggling in the classroom and seemed destined for defeat. Often these parents chose home education as a last resort. Their child's whole outlook on learning changed, and parents repeatedly share their joy of watching their child's confidence, spark, and creativity return.

Through no one individual's fault, big classrooms often set a child up for academic failure. Dr. James Dobson, psychologist and founder of Focus on the Family, shared his concern about this matter in a recent interview with home educators. He is convinced, like many parents, that much of the damaging social behavior we see in our young people today results from years of being placed into a peer pressured environment "where they cannot succeed and they cannot feel good about themselves."[1] A loving home and a nurturing parent-tutor relationship sets the stage for success.

Chapter Five

How Much Time Is Involved?

The amount of time that each family spends on actual lessons vary from home to home. Two deciding factors include the type of curriculum you are using and your child's motivation. Remember, by tutoring your child at home it is possible to adapt your routine and lesson plans to meet the needs of your child's learning style. On the average, a family can plan to spend three to five hours per day on schoolwork. Younger children will spend less, older more.

Another variable in time management will be your ability to organize, or lack of it! Be flexible enough to make room for those teachable moments that life brings your way, but don't allow yourself to be unnecessarily distracted. Prioritize and teach your children self-discipline by example. Phone calls, television, and unexpected visitors can easily cause the day to slip through your fingers if you let them. Some days just seem to go that way! However, you must make sure they become the exception and not the rule.

Even well-intentioned friends and relatives can be inconsiderate of your time. People have a tendency to assume that because you're home, you are not busy. How will they know any different if we don't set the standard ourselves. Your children are important, and their education is serious. The time you have allotted for their instruction deserves the same respect as any other full-time job. Learn to say "No," and "May I call you back?" without feeling guilty. Your child will be honored that you do!

Chapter Six

Social Short Change?

————————— ✍ —————————

One of the most widely asked questions about home education is, "Will they be normal?" This question of social development is probably the most misunderstood aspect of home education. The concern is well merited and certainly worthy of examination. We must take our children's social well-being into serious consideration, for they are our nation's future.

Recently, a study on social development was done through the University of Florida's College of Education. According to psychotherapist Larry Shyers, "The results seem to show that a child's social development depends more on adult contact and less on contact with other children than previously thought."[1] Two groups of children ages eight to ten were observed at play by trained counselors who were unaware of the educational background of the children. One group consisted of children educated at home, the other in conventional public and private classrooms. It was discovered that children taught at home, play better together and took the initiative in inviting other children to join their activities. Scores in self-concept and assertiveness were similar for both groups. However, "traditionally schooled children were considerably more aggressive, loud, and competitive than homeschooled children of the same age," reported Shyers.[2] The test results proved what homeschoolers have known all along.

Parents of school age children often find themselves unpleasantly surprised by the behavior their children pick up at school. The University of Florida study also found that children taught by their parents at home had consistently fewer behavior problems. Mr. Shyer resolves that the study "indicates that home educated children behave better because they tend to imitate their parents, while traditionally schooled children model themselves after other children in their classroom."[3] Our contemporary culture segregates children according to their ages. For their entire educational career, the vast majority of their social interaction is with other equally immature children. Then we wonder why they can't act like independent, responsible young adults upon graduation when life begins to demand that they do.

A report from the National Home Education Research Institute sheds further light on this issue. The Vineland Adaptive Behavior Scale was recently used to assess the communication, daily living skills, and socialization of children. Like the Florida studies, these composite scores revealed superior social development in home educated children. According to the report, several reasons were cited for significantly higher scores, one being

> that children taught at home are in a richer communication environment where they have instant access to the attention of a significant adult. Also the home setting encourages age integration that mirrors the larger society more so than does the conventional age segregated school.[4]

Children are natural imitators of those they are around. Peer dependent little children turn into peer dependent teen-agers, who are finding it harder and harder to grow up. Dr. Michael Platt, author and father of three, suggests that while the physiological development is quite normal and God given, the social behavior we have come to tolerate from our young people has evolved within the last few generations. In his article, "The Myth of the Teen-ager," Dr. Michael Platt describes the youth of the past:

Youths associated with other youths, sometimes dressed alike, talked alike, but never
separated entirely from their teachers and
parents. When you saw youths with their
parents, they were not pretending to be un-
related to the family. After all, they wanted
one day to become like their parents, or like
their grandparents, or like their teachers.[5]

Times have changed. Not long ago, it
was not uncommon for America's children
to be taught at home by private tutors or
parents. Even those who went to school
learned together in one-room school houses.
The public school was an extension of the
American family. The teacher upheld the
values of the parents in his or her community and was accountable to them if he or
she did not. Upon completion of their school-
ing, these young men and women were better equipped to face the challenges of everyday life. Many took on the trades of their
fathers and were productive, respectful citizens. Having been raised as godly, hard-
working people, they were prepared to give
back to their communities more than they
had been given. Thus, America thrived.

Yesterday's youths had heroes, good heroes, men and women of wisdom, valor, faith,
and integrity. They looked up to the adults
who shaped their world, not merely to each

other. Dr. Platt comments on today's modern teen-ager:

> The teen-ager has no such heroes; he may be miserable, he may not like himself, but his heroes are no more happy or worthy than himself. The highest desire of a Teen-ager is to become a more perfect Teen-ager, a Rock or movie star, certainly not a man or a woman.[6]

Peer pressure is just that, *pressure*! Pressure to perform and to conform. Your child's self-esteem and self-confidence will become evident as he exercises the freedom to learn within the security of his own family structure. At home, self-worth is not based on how well he performs, his physical looks, or the clothes he wears. He is a vital part of the family team, and no one can play his position any better!

Homeschooling is certainly not a panacea for all of our nation's social ills, and there is no way your child can avoid being exposed to the hurts and dangers of America's contemporary confusion. But teaching them at home does provide you with the opportunity to better prepare your child for real life and establish a solid foundation of biblical truth on which he or she can stand.

Chapter Seven

Support Groups

———————— ✍ ————————

Local support groups often provide a variety of enrichment activities for your child. A support group is simply a few or many families who become a network of support for each other. There may or may not be a formal membership. While some families choose not to join a support group, most find the fun and the fellowship priceless.

In large, metropolitan areas, one may find several support groups in various parts of the city. Some of these larger groups have been able to establish lending libraries, curriculum labs, and food co-ops. Some parents pool their resources and hire art, music, dance, and gymnastic instructors, or parents teach the classes themselves. Scout troops, various clubs, and sporting events can be made up entirely of children within a large group. However, the quality of the group is not restricted by the number of members. Small towns will obviously have smaller groups. While you may not have enough children to make up a ball team, you can still pool your resources together and offer a variety of activities. The whole idea is to use as many different talents within your groups as you can to nurture the talents of the children.

Community projects are something that come together well in smaller towns because everybody knows each other and knows what needs to be done. For instance, you will be doing Widow Jones a great service by picking up her leaves in the fall. You will also be giving a wonderful gift to the group of children whom you teach to work side by side in selfless service. A job that may overwhelm one person becomes a delight when others join in!

Families who live in rural areas may have to drive a bit to join in some of the activities. Most of these families are in the country because they want to be, so they don't mind the drive a bit. We began a support group in rural Mississippi with four families living thirty to sixty minutes from each other. By word of mouth, our group grew and families seemed to come out of the wood work! We simply hadn't known any other homeschoolers were around. In one year, our group has grown to over fifty families in a fifty mile radius. Not everyone is able to participate in all the activities, but it's nice to know we are here for each other if we're needed.

Science and history fairs, craft classes, picnics, field trips, drama companies, 4-H clubs, swim parties, and sports days are all wonderful cooperative activities that groups of all ages can enjoy. If your community or support group does not offer what your family is interested in, then initiate it yourself. You'd be surprised how eager others may be to join you! Clubs are especially good opportunities in leadership training for older youth.

As we mentioned earlier, support groups also serve to keep families informed of any proposed legislation that may affect them. Some states have lobbying groups. All states have prayer groups! Maladies can often be avoided by quick action and diligent prayer. Most states offer annual conferences, workshops, camps, curriculum fairs, and used book sales. Generally, local support group leaders serve to inform you of news and events.

Usually a support group starts out with the intention of providing interaction between the children, but children aren't the only ones who benefit. As parents, we often neglect our own need for fellowship. Men and women alike need to be able to share

Chapter Eight

Hey, Sports Fans!

---- ✍ ----

I realize there are some children (moms and dads, too) who are die-hard sports fans. For some families, the availability of team sports may be a deciding factor in whether or not they choose home education. Let me share with you how some families that we know of have solved this dilemma.

It is usually difficult for home educators to play team sports through their local public school, but not impossible. You may be glad to know there are other options, however. Recently, Bob Jones University Press reported that a group of homeschooled students in Georgia joined forces to form the East Metro Atlanta basketball teams.[1] Their coach, a home educator, took the initiative to contact other families. The response was tremendous. EMAC girls junior high and varsity teams were formed first. Three years later boys' teams were added. The teams, who play Christian schools in their area, have done extremely well, ending their 1990 season with a varsity record of 19-4 for the boys and 16-1 for the girls. EMAC teams placed in the consolation bracket at an annual Christian High School Invitational Basketball Tournament.

Atlanta is a big place, but it doesn't take many boys or girls to form a team. What it does take is time, effort, and determination. Many families simply opt for youth and little league teams. Church leagues are available for older youth. Bowling, hiking, skating, swimming, and volleyball are also sports that can be enjoyed by groups of almost any size.

We know of a woman who was a physical education teacher before she was a homeschool mom. She now coaches a friend's son, who is also home educated, in track. At our fall camp, the issue of statewide intramural sporting events was discussed. God is always opening new doors. Remember to seek Him first in all you do, and He will show you the way to go.

Chapter Nine

Dust or Chalk Dust?

—————————— ✍ ——————————

How is a homeschool like a school? How is it like a home? This is a difficult concept for some people to grasp. Each homeschool is as unique as each family's home, because it is just that—a home! A home which just so happens to be the center of family life and learning. Some families have actual school rooms with chalk boards, maps, desks, and even a flag! This is where they meet each day until lessons are over, and they leave, just like a conventional school. This works well for them, and they would have it no other way. I will admit it certainly must keep the rest of their home tidier. Other families have work stations. The children may have desks or a table set up near their materials, making it a natural area at which to do the bulk of their school work. This may be in a dining room or part of the living room. The majority of families I know simply use their kitchen table for math by day and dinner by night! Families who integrate their studies tend to teach all over the house, the garage, and the yard! While their children may have a desk or work area for individual studying, the nucleus of this family's school work can not be confined to any one area. This can get real messy, I'll admit, but usually the lessons are worth it.

One thing that all homeschools have in common is books—lots and lots of books! Most families are avid readers and have very well stocked personal libraries. Bookshelves become necessary pieces of furniture, and sometimes they just have to be put where they are most convenient and not necessarily where they are the most attractive!

While most states allow the freedom to decide what months you will have school and what months you will take off, many families still prefer to follow a typical schedule, with time off in the summer. We prefer to school during the hot summers and coldest part of winter. We take our breaks in spring and fall—to garden, hike, chop wood, and vacation. This is the time when our weather is nicest, and the days seem to call us out to play.

Chores are an integral part of every home. When mom becomes a full-time teacher, the children will have opportunities to learn a variety of life skills as well as academics.

Tasks can be divided up among family members according to their ages and abilities. Our two sons have been able to do their own laundry properly for some time now. Our oldest loves to cook, and what a blessing it is to have him prepare an occasional meal for the family.

Cottage industries are not uncommon among homeschool families. Family businesses are a wonderful opportunity for children to learn economics, money management, public relations, and leadership skills. Children are natural entrepreneurs, and what better way to let their creativity work than to let them start their own business! There are a few good books on the market if your family is interested in starting a business in your home.

Chapter Ten

All in a Day's Work

No two families are alike, but the best way I know of to show you what goes on during a typical day in a homeschool is to invite you to ours. Since you cannot come to us, we will come to you. Welcome to our home; we're glad you've joined us! Today is Tuesday, a typical "school day." In the past I have preferred to put my own unit studies together, but we are using conventional text books and workbooks this year. However, we still allow ourselves the privilege of plunging beyond their pages into subjects that spark our interest.

I prefer to spend the very early hour of each morning alone. For me, this is a precious, necessary time to pray, read, and be in the sweet presence of the Lord. Occasionally I will share a cup of coffee with my husband, who also enjoys his quiet mornings to prepare for his day out in the world. We encourage our three children to make this a

time of personal devotion as well. Sometimes,
if they are up early we will gather for prayer
before my husband leaves. Today they are
still asleep, and I am enjoying the quiet!

By 8:00 A.M. the children are up and
dressed, and we have breakfast together. We
make our beds, clean up the kitchen, and I
throw a load of laundry into the washer. By
9:00 A.M. we are ready to roll. Our family
chooses to start the day with prayer, singing,
and Bible study. Occasionally we still say
the pledge of allegiance. We don't hurry
through our Bible study. This is the foundation for the rest of our day, and we allow
each other and the Lord as much time as is
needed for instruction, encouragement, and
inspiration. From here we will begin our individual lessons.

I have previously written down their
daily assignments and stuck them to a wall
chart which hangs in our kitchen. I begin by
instructing our oldest, Lou, in his math,
which usually takes me about twenty minutes. Later in the day I will correct his work
and we'll go over anything he missed. Our
youngest, Maggie, is ready to do her language arts. She has been listening to a cas-
sette tape of phonics songs, and now we will
learn to write some new words. We spend
about thirty minutes together reading, writing, singing, and spelling, mostly on the liv-

ing room rug. By then she is ready for a break, and I send her off to start on her chores, which include feeding the cat outside. I'm certain she will go by way of the tire swing! Our twelve year old, Phillip, has been using the computer to type his spelling and vocabulary lessons this morning. He has already practiced his penmanship by copying a passage of scripture that has been pre-written as a model for him. Together we spend the next half hour together going over yesterday's English assignment and today's instructions. We drill his spelling words and he goes to his desk in his room. He will finish his lesson and take a math test.

By now, Lou has finished his math and already started his English lesson, which is a review of business letters. He is writing to a company requesting information on a model he is interested in building. I sit with Maggie as she reads to me from her library book. We memorize a poem and tell knock-knock jokes as she helps me start lunch. The boys are still working, so she and I do her math while they finish.

We do not hurry through lunch today. It is a good time to make afternoon plans and decide who will do what chores when we are finished eating. Our oldest reads me his business letter and asks me to critique it. The laundry gets hung and the table cleared once

again. I check the boys math papers with
them. On nice days, we occasionally take the
rest of our lessons to the park to finish then
hike along the nature trail. Today we will
stay home.

Lou is now in the den doing his typing
lesson on the computer. Maggie is working
on a craft project beside me at the kitchen
table as we listen to Phillip read his science
lesson. When he is finished reading, the three
of us discuss it. His older brother joins us as
we all do the accompanying experiment.
Phillip records his data and writes his con-
clusion. Lou has come up with his own
theory, alters the experiment, and compares
the results. He then sits down to his own
science book to study. I review Phillip's social studies lesson with him, which is about
France. Tonight we plan to watch *A Tale of
Two Cities*, which is about the French Revolution. Phillip offers to drill Maggie on her
continents, oceans, and the Great Lakes. He
shows her where France is, and helps her
trace it from his book.

In the meantime, I spend some time with
Lou. We studied our state history, law, and
civics last semester, and he enjoys having
the time to concentrate on his science now. It
is now a little after two o'clock. Lou still has
vocabulary words to finish and two math
problems to correct. I am free to plan

tomorrow's lessons, finish my housework, make phone calls, etc. Perhaps we'll take a walk later, go to the library, or play scrabble. Two of the children have been finished with school for nearly thirty minutes, but as you see, there is a very fine line between home and school, so fine in fact it is all but invisible.

Chapter Eleven

Where Do We Find Our Books?

———————— ✍ ————————

A vast array of curriculum is now available to home educators. Excellent Christian textbooks, workbooks, resource books, videos, cassettes, computer software, educational games, art projects, and toys are on the market, with new material being added all the time. Many of these learning tools are designed by home educators, for home educators. A brief list of resources is included in the back of this booklet.

Leafing through catalogs is fun for the whole family, but when it comes to deciding on which curriculum to choose, you may feel a little overwhelmed. For this reason, we would like to help you understand what some of your options are. It would be impossible here to review all of the resources available, but we can discuss different types of curriculum and some advantages and disadvantages to each of them.

Correspondence Courses

Some states require home educators to be registered under a certified private school. Many private schools across America have spread open their wings to accommodate us. They offer correspondence courses for all grade levels. Other families choose this option, not for the coverage, but because they like having someone to be accountable to, and they like the help they receive from the school. Different correspondence schools use different types of curriculum. When choosing a course of study, consider your child's learning style as well as the cost. Most of these schools offer testing, grading, and recordkeeping services. Complete lesson plans, answer keys, and test banks are also available. In addition to curriculum, you will have registration and yearly tuition fees to pay as well. Many families find this a small price to pay for the amount of service provided.

Textbooks

Most of us attended public or private schools using the conventional teacher-directed textbook method. A typical routine went something like this: our teacher would introduce our new chapter, we would read a lesson, answer the questions, discuss our answers, and be tested on Friday. Remember? The only interruption of this format would be an occasional science experiment or snowy day! Most of the things we learned that way have long since escaped us. A good teacher will bring life to even the palest page and most boring subject. Hopefully, we all have memories of a teacher like that, one who sparked our interest and made learning fun. Most textbooks were designed for classroom use. While the content may be excellent, you will want to tailor the teaching method and lesson plans to meet your child's needs. You may want to purchase all your subjects from the same publisher or use a variety of publishers. Learning together at home allows your family the freedom to get as creative as you dare.

More companies than ever are now catering to the homeschool. By condensing some of the bulky classroom materials, they are making their products cost effective for families. Textbooks and accompanying material can be purchased from several different publishers, Christian as well as secular. Keep in mind that while this conventional method of teaching may be most familiar to you, it may not work best for your family. One reason is that, this method tends to isolate subjects from one another. Your child may be studying about volcanos in science,

Columbus in history, verbs in English, silent *e* words in spelling, and Helen Keller in reading. This certainly covers a variety of topics and appears to be offering a broad scope of learning. But in fact, your child may be retaining less material than if some of these subjects complimented each other.

If you are using this conventional method for several children in different grade levels, you can see how it may overwhelm you. I'm not suggesting we shy away from textbooks, on the contrary! In fact, some textbook companies, like Bob Jones University Press, offer lesson plans that will help you use their curriculum in multi-level teaching. However, we must keep in mind that individual children learn differently, and we need to stay flexible.

This is where we, as educators, must not be afraid to take hold of the reigns and determine who is master and who is slave! You control the curriculum; don't let it control you. To become a slave to our lesson plans can cause us to lose sight of the very essence of education. Joy will soon fade, and creativity will be sacrificed on the altar of deadlines and monotony. We must work within a frame work of order without becoming so rigid that we can no longer enjoy what we're doing.

With a little creativity, you can cut the chances in half of getting into a rut. Carefully examine the table of contents in each grade level of the same subject and propose teaching lessons of the same topic together whenever you can. Teach subjects that complement one another simultaneously. Perhaps you are learning to write reports and studying about the pony express in history. Is there a chapter on horses in your science book? Study them together. Now you have something worth writing a report on! Tie in other subjects. Ask your child, "Can you use as many spelling words as possible in that report? How about using some really strong adjectives like we learned last week?"

Now a trip to a stable might just top this week off! Have your child calculate how long it would take a rider to get from your home to the stable if he were riding a horse at full gallop. Now, determine the difference in time between riding and driving a car at 50 m.p.h. How long does it take your mail carrier? That's just sneaking in a little math to further reinforce your lesson. Math is applicable; it doesn't end just because the math book is closed. Math, like language and reasoning skills, is used for life. Don't be afraid to make it fun!

If you have more than one child, textbooks become an investment. Initially, the cost of books can seem rather high, but as the books are re used by younger children in following years, you actually begin to cut down on your purchases. You may still want to purchase individual activity books to enhance your lesson, but they are not costly. The money you save can then be used for resources or science equipment for the whole family. If and when you decide to change curriculum, you can always trade or sell your used curriculum to another homeschool!

Self-Instructional Workbooks

A popular method of study, especially among older students, is the self-paced, or accelerated learning method. Several different publishers offer a complete course of study by means of individual workbooks that the student progresses through at his own pace. Diagnostic testing is available to determine where your child would start in each subject. With each workbook, you and your child will set a goal for date of completion. Your child will then pace himself each day to attain that goal. He or she will be required to take self-examinations along the way, and you will check his or her progress. You will also administer a final exam before he or she can move on to the next workbook.

Teacher/student interaction varies with each company. There is a minimal amount of teacher preparation, and in some cases you will act as a monitor rather than an actual instructor. As with any curriculum, it is up to you whether you will use it exclusively or only for certain subjects.

Unit Studies

The recognition of unit studies is gaining momentum even in conventional schools. Children learn best when they are actively involved in their educational process. Too many times a child's eyes are on his book, his hands are busy elsewhere, and his heart and mind are out on the playground. What he reads today is often forgotten by tomorrow. It is a known fact that we retain information in direct proportion to how many of our senses we use to process it. Unit studies not only get your entire child involved in the learning process but also incorporate as many subjects as possible. They are put together using textbooks, as we did with the pony express lesson, as well as a variety of other resources. Our own unit studies involved videos or films, cooking, textbooks, art, music, drama, story writing, literature, map skills, field trips, science projects, and lots and lots of library books!

Several well-planned and completely laid out unit studies are on the market today. Most are written by very creative home educators, who have taken the time to share their ideas. These will cover the basic scope of academic skills, yet the sequence in which they are taught will vary.

Teaching unit studies usually costs the least amount of money but the most amount of time. The money you save on texts and workbooks allows you to purchase all the necessary extras that make your unit study unique, exciting, and memorable. It is essential that you plan carefully and budget for your supplies and activities, however the actual cost of each unit is up to you.

Unit studies require discipline on your part. A great deal of preparation is involved. Be honest with yourself, but don't limit yourself either. Many parents find this method of teaching overwhelming. It needn't be, and it can even be quite an advantage to families with several children. Getting involved with another homeschool family, if properly done, can cut the work in half and be twice the fun!

Unit studies are an excellent means by which to impart knowledge, apply skills, and retain what you learn. If you decide to use units prepared by someone else, remember, there is always room for your own individual ideas. The Spirit of the Creator lives in you and He knows what is best for your family. Seek Him with all your heart, and don't limit Him!

Videos

Video schools are another option. These are available through certain accredited Christian schools as well as individual companies. There are several obvious advantages to video courses. In most cases, a regular classroom teacher is videotaped while teaching his or her class. Your child receives the same formal instruction a public school class does. Assignments are given, and math, spelling, and vocabulary drills are done together. Many parents choose this option once their children reach high school age and subjects become more involved. In most circumstances, video courses are rented for the duration of the school year and remain the property of the school. For this reason they can not be used again by upcoming students. Rental, book, and postage fees must also be considered. Video courses can be very convenient but very costly as well.

No matter what method of teaching you choose, remember that all of these materials are simply tools, and no single curriculum is perfect. There are many books, games, and programs for every grade level and subject. What may work for one family may be all wrong for another. Listen to the wisdom of others who are more experienced, and learn from their mistakes. Always pray, and don't be afraid to try things for yourself if you feel led. It may be just what you need.

In some ways children are a lot alike, but each one is precious and unique with strengths and weaknesses that will become more apparent to you as you spend time together. Two undeniable advantages you have in teaching your own children is that you love them, and more than anything else, you want them to succeed.

I think our greatest reward of all in choosing to home educate has been our growth as a family, in our relationship with the Lord, and in love towards one another. We truly enjoy each other, and our family is enriched every year. Days do not always go smoothly, attitudes are not always right, and plans do get altered. But as we learn to lean on God and walk in His ways, His grace abounds, and we are strengthened.

Oh yes! There is one last question yet to cover! "What **do** I tell my mother-in-law?" Unfortunately, I get asked this question a lot, and I hear it from both husbands **and** wives. I regret that our own parents live so far away. That limits our access to their wisdom and talents. I am very grateful for the interest, encouragement, support, and contributions from my parents, but many teaching moms are not so blessed.

Perhaps it is not only your parents, but neighbors, relatives, or close friends that voice their concerns about "this crazy idea of yours" to home educate. Listen to their concerns and seriously pray about what they say, especially if they have given you godly counsel in the past. If the Lord is truly leading your family in this direction, and you and your spouse are in agreement, then don't be afraid to take that step. Whom God calls, He also equips. You are accountable to God, and He will give you His grace to walk in that obedience. He will also give you the grace to properly respond to opposition.

Try to remember that your loved ones only have your best interest at heart. Most of the time their fears simply stem from lack of information about home education. We're never too old to learn. Share with them the information you have just read. Pray that God would show them His will and, above all, keep a right attitude.

It may be that they are waiting to see some fruit before they will be convinced. Ask God to show you how you can involve them in your homeschool in a way that will bless everyone. No one can enrich a history lesson, a nature walk, or a woodworking class like a grandparent. Trust Him, do your best, and let the results speak for themselves!

May God be with each of you as you enter into a most challenging, joyful adventure. Get ready, life may never be the same! Remember: "Trust in the Lord with all of your heart and lean not to your own understanding. Acknowledge Him in all of your ways and He will keep your path straight."

Proverbs 3:6

Notes

Chapter Two

1. Dr. Brian Ray, *The Teaching Home* (Oct/Nov. 1992): 26.

2. Dr. Raymond Moore, *Home Style Teaching* (Waco, TX: Word Books, 1984), 181.

Chapter Three

1. Gary H. Kah, *En Route to Global Occupation* (Lafayette, LA: Huntington House Publishers, 1992), 60.

2. Eugene H. Methvin, "Guess Who Spells Disaster for Education," *Reader's Digest* (Reprint May 1984): 3.

3. Ibid., 4.

4. Mike Fuselier, *America Awaiting the Verdict* (Lafayette, LA: Huntington House Publishers, 1992).

Chapter Four

1. Dr. James Dobson, Turn Your Heart Toward Home-radio Broadcast Focus on the Family (Colorado Springs, CO: 4 February 1993).

Chapter Six

1. AP, Gainsville, Fla. "Study compares school kids with those taught at home," *Daily Sentinel Star* (17 July 1992).

2. Ibid.

3. Ibid.

4. Dr. Brian Ray, "Research on Socialization Rates Home Schoolers High," *The Teaching Home* (December 1992/January 1993): 21.

5. Dr. Michael Platt, "The Myth of the Teenager," *Practical Homeschooling* vol. 1, no. 2 (Summer 1993):19.

6. Ibid.

Chapter Eight

1. "The Home Court Advantage," *Home School Helper*, vol. 4, no. 3 (BJU Press, 1990): 2.

Resources

The following list of educational resources is by no means exhaustive. New products are being added daily. We hope families who are new to home education will find the following information helpful and a good place to start. Call or write to request catalogs, samples, or further information. For reviews on a variety of products, we recommend *Mary Pride's Big Book of Home Learning*. This four volume set will give you a run down on just about every curriculum on the market.

Periodicals

The Teaching Home Magazine
P.O. Box 20219
Portland, OR 97220-0219

Homeschooling Today
P.O. Box 1425
Melrose, FL 32666

Practical Homeschooling
P.O. Box 1250
Fenton, MO 63026-1850

God's World Publication
Box 2330
Asheville, NC 28802
1-800-951-5437

Family Research Council
700 Thirteenth St. NW Suite 500
Washington, D.C. 20005

Unit Studies

The Cornerstone Project
2006 Flat Creek
Richardson, TX 75080

The Weaver Curriculum
2752 Scarborough
Riverside, CA 92503

KONOS
P.O. Box 1534
Richardson, TX 75083

Phonics Programs

Play & Talk
7105 Manzanita St.
Carlsbad, CA 92009
1-800-472-7525

Sing Spell Read & Write

1-800-472-7525

General

Abeka
1-800-874-3592

ACE
1-800-622-3070

Alpha Omega
1-800-622-3070

Bob Jones University Press
1-800-845-5731

Saxon Math
1320 W. Lindsey
Norman, OK 73069

More Good Books From
HUNTINGTON HOUSE PUBLISHERS

RECENT RELEASES

Trojan Horse—
How the New Age Movement Infiltrates
the Church
by Samantha
Smith & Brenda Scott

New Age/Occult concepts and techniques are being introduced into all major denominations. The revolution is subtle, cumulative, and deadly. Through what door has this heresy entered the church? Authors Samantha Smith and Brenda Scott attempt to demonstrate that Madeleine L'Engle has been and continues to be a major New Age source of entry into the church. Because of her radical departure from traditional Christian theology, Madeleine L'Engle's writings have sparked a wave of controversy across the nation. She has been published and promoted by numerous magazines, including *Today's Christian Woman*, *Christianity Today* and others. The deception, unfortunately, has been so successful that otherwise discerning congregations and pastors have fallen into the snare that has been laid.

Sadly, many Christians are embracing the demonic doctrines of the New Age movement. Well hidden under "Christian" labels, occult practices, such as Zen meditation, altered states, divinations, out of body experences, "discovering the Divine truth within" and others have defiled many. This book explores the depths of infiltration and discusses ways to combat it.

ISBN 56384-040-5 $9.99

Don't Touch That Dial: The Impact of the Media on

Children and the Family

by Barbara Hattemer & Robert Showers

Men and women without any stake in the outcome of the war between the pornographers and our families have come to the qualified, professional agreement that media does have an effect on our children—an effect that is devastatingly significant. Highly respected researchers, psychologists, and sociologists join a bevy of pediatricians, district attorneys, parents, teachers, pastors, and community leaders—who have diligently remained true to the fight against pornographic media—in their latest comprehensive critique of the modern media establishment (i.e., film, television, print, art, curriculum).

ISBN 1-56384-032-4 Trade Paper $9.99

ISBN 1-56384-035-9 Hardcover $19.99

When the Wicked Seize a City
by Chuck & Donna McIlhenny with Frank York

A highly publicized lawsuit . . . a house fire-bombed in the night . . . the shatter of windows smashed by politically (and wickedly) motivated vandals cuts into the night. . . . All this because Chuck McIlhenny voiced God's condemnation of a behavior and lifestyle and protested the destruction of society that results from its practice. That behavior is homosexuality, and that life-style is the gay culture. This book explores: the rise of gay power and what it will mean if Christians do not organize and prepare for the battle.

ISBN 1-56384-024-3 $9.99

Subtle Serpent: New Age in the Classroom
by Darylann Whitemarsh & Bill Reisman

There is a new morality being taught to our children in public schools. Without the consent or even awareness of parents— educators and social engineers are aggressively introducing new moral codes to our children. In most instances, these new moral codes contradict traditional values. Darylann Whitemarsh (a 1989 Teacher of the Year recipient) and Bill Reisman (educator and expert on the occult) combine their knowledge to expose the deliberate madness occurring in our public schools.

ISBN 1-56384-016-2 $9.99

The Extermination of Christianity
A Tyranny of Consensus
by Paul Schenck with Robert L. Schenck

Here is convincing evidence that a militant and secular coalition is using every available means to purge Christianity from off American landscape. If you are a Christian, you might be shocked to discover that:

*Popular music, television, and motion pictures are consistently depicting you as a stooge, a hypocrite, a charlatan, a racist, an anti-Semite, or a con artist;

*You could be expelled from a public high school for giving Christian literature to a classmate;

*You could be arrested and jailed for praying on school grounds.

This book is a catalogue of anti-Christian propaganda—a record of persecution before it happens!

ISBN 1-56384-051-0 $9.99

Political Correctness: The Cloning of the American Mind
by David Thibodaux, Ph.D.

The author, a professor of literature at the University of Southwestern Louisiana, confronts head on the movement that is now being called Political Correctness. Political correctness, says Thibodaux, "is an umbrella under which advocates of civil rights, gay and lesbian rights, feminism, and environmental causes have gathered." To incur the wrath of these groups, one only has to disagree with

A Jewish Conservative Looks at Pagan America

by Don Feder

With eloquence and insight that rival contemporary commentators and essayists of antiquity, Don Feder's pen finds his targets in the enemies of God, family, and American tradition and morality. Deftly . . . delightfully . . . the master allegorist and Titian with a typewriter brings clarity to the most complex sociological issues and invokes giggles and wry smiles from both followers and foes. Feder is Jewish to the core, and he finds in his Judaism no inconsistency with an American Judeo-Christian ethic. Questions of morality plague school administrators, district court judges, senators, congressmen, parents, and employers; they are wrestling for answers in a "changing world." Feder challenges this generation and directs inquirers to the original books of wisdom: the Torah and the Bible.

ISBN 1-56384-036-7 Trade Paper $9.99

ISBN 1-56384-037-5 Hardcover $19.99

Kinsey, Sex and Fraud:
The Indoctrination of a People
by *Dr. Judith A. Reisman and Edward Eichel*

Kinsey, Sex and Fraud describes the research of Alfred Kinsey which shaped Western society's beliefs and understanding of the
nature of human sexuality. His unchallenged
conclusions are taught at every level of
education—elementary, high school and
college—and quoted in textbooks as undis-
puted truth.

The authors clearly demonstrate that
Kinsey's research involved illegal experimen-
tations on several hundred children. The
survey was carried out on a non-representa-
tive group of Americans, including dispropor-
tionately large numbers of sex offenders,
prostitutes, prison inmates and exhibitionists.

ISBN 0-910311-20-X $10.99

"Soft Porn" Plays Hardball
by *Dr. Judith A. Reisman*

With amazing clarity, the author demon-
strates that pornography imposes on society a
view of women and children that encourages
violence and sexual abuse. As crimes against
women and children increase to alarming
proportions, it's of paramount importance
that we recognize the cause of this violence.
Pornography should be held accountable for
the havoc it has wreaked in our homes and
our country.

ISBN 0-910311-65-X Trade Paper $8.99
ISBN 0-910311-92-7 Hardcover $16.95

ORDER THESE HUNTINGTON HOUSE BOOKS !

——*A Call to Manhood: In a Fatherless Society— $9.99——
David E. Long

——*Conservative, American, and Jewish—Jacob   9.99——
Neusner

——Deadly Deception: Freemasonry—Tom   8.99——
McKenney

——*Don't Touch That Dial—Barbara Hattemer &   9.99/——
Robert Showers (Hardcover also available)   19.99

——En Route to Global Occupation—Gary Kah   9.99——

——*The Extermination of Christianity—Paul   9.99——
Schenck w/Robert L.Schenck

——*Gays & Guns—John Eidsmoe   7.99/14.99——

——*A Generation Betrayed—Randy Kirk   9.99——

——*Heresy Hunters—Jim Spencer   8.99——

——Inside the New Age Nightmare—Randall Baer   9.99——

——*I Shot an Elephant in My Pajamas: The   12.99——
Morrie Ryskind Story—Morrie Ryskind/John
Roberts

——*A Jewish Conservative Looks at Pagan   9.99/19.99——
America—Don Feder (Hardcover Available)

——*The Liberal Contradiction—Dale A. Berryhill 9.99——

——*Loyal Opposition—John Eidsmoe   8.99——

——Political Correctness—David Thibodaux   9.99——

——*Prescription Death—Dr. Reed Bell/Frank   9.99——
York

——*Real Men—Dr. Harold Voth   9.99——

——*Spying on the Enemy's Camp—Sal Dena w/   9.99——
Laura England

* *New Title*   Shipping and Handling   ——
                  Total   ——

AVAILABLE AT BOOKSTORES EVERY WHERE or order
direct from: Huntington House Publishers • P.O. Box 53788 •
Lafayette, LA 70505. Send check/money order. For faster
service use VISA/MASTERCARD call toll-free 1-800-749-4009.
Add: Freight and handling, $3.50 for the first book ordered,
and $.50 for each additional book up to 5 books.

Enclosed is $_____ including postage.

VISA/Mastercard # _____ Exp. Date_____

Name _____

Address _____

City, State, Zip_____

them on political, moral, or social issues. To express traditionally Western concepts in universities today can result in not only ostracism, but even suspension. (According to a recent "McNeil-Lehrer News Hour" report, one student was suspended for discussing the reality of the moral law with an avowed homosexual. He was reinstated only after he apologized.)

ISBN 1-56384-026-X Trade Paper $9.99

Loyal Opposition:
A Christian Response to the Clinton Agenda
by John Eidsmoe, Ph.D.

The night before the November 1992 elections, a well-known evangelist claims to have had a dream. In this dream, he says, God told him that Bill Clinton would be elected President, and Christians should support his Presidency. What are we to make of this? Does it follow that, because God allowed Clinton to be President; therefore, God wants Clinton to be president? Does God want everything that God allows? Is it possible for an event to occur even though that event displeases God? How do we stand firm in our opposition to the administration's proposals when those proposals contradict Biblical values? And how do we organize and work effectively for constructive action to restore our nation to basic values?

ISBN 1-56384-044-8 $8.99